D0524110

THE COOKING CANON
Rev. John Eley

BRITISH BROADCASTING
CORPORATION

D.G.R.

Thanks for the inspiration

Cover photograph taken by Bob Komar in the
Smallbone Kitchens showroom, 72 Gloucester Road,
London SW7

Published by the British Broadcasting Corporation,
35 Marylebone High Street, London W1M 4AA

ISBN 0 563 20259 9

First published 1984
© John Eley 1984

Set in 10/11pt Times by Ace Filmsetting, Frome,
Somerset and printed by Robert Hartnoll Limited,
Bodmin, Cornwall

Contents

The Versatile Pig

Some Lamb Dishes

Poultry and Game

Two Recipes for Pastry

Puddings . . . The Last Word?

Introduction

I am by nature an enthusiastic cook, not a great one or a gourmet chef. However, I do hold to certain hard and fast rules about food and cooking. It is to be enjoyed and shared, whenever possible, with others. Although I am single, I try never to eat all my meals alone each day and, of course, being a clergyman, I have more scope than most people for meeting new friends and inviting them in for a meal.

Sitting down together at a common meal, no matter how simple, is more than just a politeness offered to a friend or stranger – it helps in the art of communication and in breaking down barriers. Eating is probably one of the most private things that we do in public, refuelling ourselves for the tasks of the day. It was not by chance that Jesus held a last supper with his friends. The act of sharing in breaking bread together has been with us for centuries. The Bedouin sees hospitality to the stranger as one of his most important duties, and St Benedict had a few fine things to say about hospitality as well. However, it saddens me to see how many families are less and less able to sit down to a meal together each day, or at least once a week. It does take an effort and discipline, but I believe it is worth it.

The kitchen can so easily become the most important room in the house and is often the most neglected. It's funny how people frequently find it easier to talk about their problems and their joys when I am talking with them in the kitchen as we wait for the kettle to boil or I prepare something to eat. You are giving yourself to the other person by giving them your time. One of the privileges of being a clergyman is that, although we are busy people, our time is mostly spent with other people in a way that is not possible with many other professions.

Enough of this serious business. Back to the cooking. My palate could be described as having the 'common touch' since a lot of the dishes I prepare seem to find a certain amount of popularity. If we all tried to do a painting of the same scene, the resulting pictures would be very different although the fundamentals remain the same . . . and so it is with cooking, I feel. We each put our signature on everything we do.

I hope that those of you who are curious enough to try some of the dishes in this little cookery book will find delight in them, for food is an adventure and why journey alone? Take a friend along with you.

Happy Cooking

God bless

John

(A very special word of thanks to all those kind people who send me recipes, and my good friends who make useful suggestions and provide me with tasty ideas.)

Conversion Tables

All these are approximate conversions which have either been rounded up or down. Never mix imperial and metric measures in one recipe, stick to one system or the other.

Oven temperature

Mark 1	275°F	140°C
2	300°	150°
3	325°	170°
4	350°	180°
5	375°	190°
6	400°	200°
7	425°	220°
8	450°	230°
9	475°	240°

Volume

2 fl oz	55 ml
3	75
5 ($\frac{1}{4}$ pt)	150
$\frac{1}{2}$ pt	275
$\frac{3}{4}$	425
1	570
$1\frac{3}{4}$	1 litre

Measurements

$\frac{1}{8}$ inch	3 mm
$\frac{1}{4}$	$\frac{1}{2}$ cm
$\frac{1}{2}$	1
$\frac{3}{4}$	2
1	2.5
$1\frac{1}{4}$	3
$1\frac{1}{2}$	4
$1\frac{3}{4}$	4.5
2	5
3	7.5
4	10
5	13
6	15
7	18
8	20
9	23
10	25.5
11	28
12	30

Weights

$\frac{1}{2}$ oz	10 g
1	25
$1\frac{1}{2}$	40
2	50
$2\frac{1}{2}$	60
3	75
4	110
$4\frac{1}{2}$	125
5	150
6	175
7	200
8	225
9	250
10	275
12	350
1 lb	450
$1\frac{1}{2}$	700
2	900
3	1 kg 350 g

Soups and Starters

The habit, rather than the art, of making soup seems to have given way to the can-opener. Yet we are all capable of reversing that process. There is nothing complicated here, so do go ahead and try them.

Sweetcorn Soup

I'm always grateful when people write in to me with their favourite recipes. This one comes from an appreciative viewer of the second *Pebble Mill At One* series I did. I've tried it and agree with her it's delicious. Thank you, Cary Holyoake of Maidenhead.

1 tin sweetcorn	1 oz flour
1 medium onion	4 oz bacon
1 pint milk	Chopped nuts and
1 pint chicken stock	cream to garnish
1 oz butter	

Finely chop the bacon and fry until the fat is sweated out. Put on one side. Finely chop the onion and fry lightly in the butter until soft. Add flour, cook for one minute and remove from heat. Add the sweetcorn, milk and stock and return to stove to simmer for one minute. Liquidise in the food processor. Reheat, and serve garnished with the finely chopped bacon, nuts and a little soured cream.

This freezes extremely well.

Peanut Soup

Another suggestion from a viewer. I had heard of this soup some years ago but never managed to trace a recipe. It has its origins in Kenya in 1928. My thanks to Mary Heat of Cheltenham for passing it on to me.

½ lb peanuts
1 onion
1 stick of celery
3 cups white stock
1 pint milk

1 oz butter
1 oz flour
2 oz cream
Salt and pepper

Put the nuts in a pan with the chopped onion, celery and milk. Simmer for one hour. Melt butter and flour and cook slightly. Add the stock and boil, stirring all the time. Add the rest of the milk and the nuts. Boil again and add cream and seasoning before serving.

Oatmeal Posset

When I was first handed this recipe some years ago, I rushed for the *Oxford English Dictionary* to find out what a posset actually is. I thought it was a furry creature from down-under but was relieved to find that it is a drink of curdled milk and ale suitable for the curing of colds. The recipe has its origins north of the Border, as you may well have guessed. It was given to me by Mrs Diana Brown of Heversham.

1 pint milk
Pinch of nutmeg and
   cinnamon
2 tbsp oatmeal flour

3 tbsp dry white wine
3 tbsp light ale
2 tbsp raw cane sugar

Boil the milk flavoured with nutmeg and cinnamon. Stir in oatmeal flour and simmer for 2 minutes. Mix together the wine, ale and sugar. Bring to boil and pour over the milk. Simmer gently for 1 minute and pour into serving jug. Cover and allow to stand for a short while before serving.

Schnoosch

As I've already remarked, being a clergyman means that you have easy access to people. And working in a cathedral means that you meet many passers-by who sometimes surprise you with their culinary talents. Schnoosch is the result of a happy encounter with a student doctor from Germany who was on a three months' locum with us at the Cumberland Infirmary. I met him one day after Evensong in the cathedral and invited him to join the mad party that seems to run unabated around the house. We have been firm friends ever since. So try Schnoosch for friendship's sake. It is a delicious vegetable soup that can be served as a starter but acts just as well as a luncheon dish.

Use ½ lb each of the following vegetables:

Carrots	Turnips
Green beans	Sprouts
Parsnips	Swede
Peas (fresh or frozen)	

You will also need:

1½ pints milk	2 slices smoked bacon
2 tbsp potato flour	per person
1 dessertspoon sugar	

Cube all the root vegetables. Cook the vegetables in the usual way with a little salted water. Meanwhile scald 1½ pints of milk. Strain the vegetables and add to the milk with a couple of tablespoons of potato flour and a dessertspoon of sugar. Simmer until the liquid begins to thicken.

Meanwhile, grill two slices of smoked bacon for each person and serve the soup hot with the grilled bacon on a side plate.

I knew you would be surprised.

Virgin Mary's Soup

For obvious reasons I could not forget this recipe which was handed to me by the wife of an American Air Force pilot some years ago in Suffolk. They had good cause to remember me. But more of that later.

4 eggs	5 fluid oz double cream
1½ pints of good stock	Salt
3 oz breadcrumbs	White pepper
1 cooked chicken breast	Croutons of white bread
3 oz peeled blanched almonds	

Hard boil the eggs and keep the yolks only. Boil together one-third of the stock and the breadcrumbs, and add to a food processor along with the chicken breast and almonds. Process for a few seconds and then add the cream, salt and pepper to taste, and process again. In a double boiler keep this mixture warm until the rest of the stock has been heated up, and then add to the stock.

Be careful in heating this dish as the purée may curdle.

Serve with white bread croutons.

Mystery Mousse

Ruth Graysbrooke's little cottage in Sherborne, Dorset, has been the scene of many happy meals for me. Here is a very simple starter that we had at our very first meeting. I have never forgotten it.

1 tin beef consommé	$\frac{1}{2}$ tsp curry powder
1 small packet Philadelphia cheese	Capers for garnish

Blend together all the ingredients thoroughly. Pour into ramekins and chill well until set. Garnish with a caper or two.

Serve well chilled, with some slices of brown bread and butter.

Lunch and Suppertime Snacks

Here are a few versatile dishes that can be served at lunchtime, suppertime, or at any time. They are the sort of dishes that I like to serve up in the early evening after Evensong, when I may have some people in before going off together for some diocesan committee meeting or other. Usually, such dishes can be timed to cook during Evensong, provided it is not the fifteenth evening of the month when the psalms go on for ever!

Lymeswold Cheese Flan

I have Mrs Diana Burra to thank for this recipe. It is one she entered for the Great Cumbria Cookery Competition some months ago. I was one of the judges, and when I tasted this it really took my fancy. It is rumoured that Lymeswold is very hard to get hold of – is this because of its popularity or its under-production? – but it is worth tracking down for this flan, which is delicious. It could perhaps be made as well with a piece of Stilton.

8 oz shortcrust pastry	$\frac{1}{2}$ pint single cream
6 oz cubed ham	Salt and pepper
6 oz Lymeswold cheese	1 tbsp chopped parsley
1 onion, finely chopped	1 oz butter
3 eggs	

Line a flan case with the pastry and sprinkle the ham over the base.

Gently sauté the finely chopped onion in the butter, and remove from the heat. Beat together the eggs, cream and crumbled cheese, adding salt and pepper and the chopped parsley. Pour this mixture over the cubed ham and bake in a moderate oven at gas mark 5, 375°F (190°C), for about 40 minutes.

This is richly flavoured and can be served either hot or cold.

Tuesday Pie

I am assured that this is a favourite dish of Jemma, Karen, Tabitha and Ruth as well as Jill, head cook and bottlewasher at the Vicarage at Grayshott in Surrey. Thank you very much. It is on my list now, and very enjoyable it is, too.

1 lb cooked brown rice	1 6 oz tin salmon
8 oz cooked peas, French beans, sweetcorn and diced peppers	1 clove garlic

Cheese sauce
1 oz butter   6 oz toasted oats
1 oz plain flour
6 oz grated Cheddar
  cheese

Butter an ovenproof dish. Mix together the rice, vegetables, salmon and chopped garlic. Pour into the dish. Make up the rich cheese sauce and pour over the rice mixture. Sprinkle the toasted oats on top and bake in a slow oven, gas mark 3, 325°F (170°C) for about an hour.

Serve this dish with broccoli and grilled tomatoes.

Cumberland Sausage Bake

I thought this dish had been around for years, but when I gave it to some Cumbrian friends a few weeks ago I was surprised to discover none of them had come across it before. Their great pleasure at tasting it has encouraged me to include it for you. If you cannot get hold of Cumberland sausage, your local butcher's best sausages should make an acceptable substitute.

1 lb Cumberland sausage, or other sausages

1 lb cooking apples
1 large onion

Cheese sauce
1 pint milk
1 oz butter
1 oz plain flour

4 oz Cheddar cheese
1 oz Parmesan cheese

Place the sausage and onion together in an ovenproof dish. Cover with finely grated apple. Make up the cheese sauce in the usual way. Pour over the apple and sausage and bake in a hot oven, gas mark 6, 400°F (200°C), for 15–20 minutes.

Serve with baked jacket potatoes.

Potato and Artichoke Pie

Thank heaven for nuns, especially French nuns! I am a regular visitor to Le Bec Hellouin in Normandy, which is for me always a fascinating place. At one end of the village there is le monastère, where the nuns live, and at the other end, l'abbé, where the monks live. Hospitality being the very nature of a Benedictine abbey, and because the food is so excellent there, I usually elect to stay with the nuns.

This is one of their many superb vegetable dishes.

1½ lb cooked new potatoes	1 lb artichoke hearts (or use tinned hearts)

1¼ pints of rich cheese sauce made with:

2 oz butter	6 oz Gruyère cheese, grated
2 oz plain flour	
1 pint milk	salt and pepper

Cook the potatoes and the artichokes and place in a large ovenproof dish. Make up the cheese sauce by melting the butter in a thick saucepan and adding the flour gradually until it is cooked. Then add the milk gradually, and finally the cheese. Season with some salt and pepper. Pour the sauce over the artichokes and pop into a moderate oven at about gas mark 5, 375°F (190°C), for about 20 minutes.

A tasty lunchtime dish.

Quiche Lorraine

I get very depressed by some of the things that are served up in restaurants and cafés in this country under the name of Quiche Lorraine. They are usually a disaster. *This* is the true Quiche Lorraine. I have not made a mistake by leaving out the cheese – there *is* no cheese in a true Quiche Lorraine: the Parisians were responsible for that particular unnecessary extravagance. Try it like this. I'm sure you won't regret it.

8 oz shortcrust pastry	4 eggs
½ pint double cream	Salt and pepper
6 oz smoked gammon, cubed	

In a frying pan sweat the gammon so that the excess fat runs off. Allow to cool.

Beat together well three whole eggs and the yolk of the fourth, together with ample salt and pepper.

Line a 10-inch flan tin with the short crust pastry and sprinkle the gammon over the base. Pour over the cream and egg mixture. Bake in a moderate oven, gas mark 5, 375°F (190°C), for 35 to 40 minutes and serve immediately.

I like to serve this for supper straight from the oven with a green salad.

Braised Red Cabbage

We come now to the first of three dishes from the continent. This recipe for Braised Red Cabbage was given to me by Elizabeth Crookenden. I am grateful to her for unearthing it for me. Do try it, for it really is in a class of its own. It is German in origin.

2–2½ lb red cabbage
2 medium-sized onions
2 large cooking apples
 (Bramleys if you can
 get them)
Butter or goose fat

1 glass of good red wine
 or port
1 tbsp demerara sugar
Salt and pepper
1 tbsp wine vinegar
Thyme

Remove the stalk and outer leaves from the red cabbage. Shred the main part. Chop the onion and slice, peel and core the apples. Melt about 2 heaped tablespoons of the fat in a thick saucepan and build up layers of cabbage, onion and apple, sprinkling on salt, pepper and sugar as you go. Pour over the wine and the vinegar. Seal the lid of the pan with some greaseproof paper and simmer for an hour to an hour and a half, remembering to stir gently from time to time. Towards the end of the cooking time, add about a teaspoon of thyme or a sprig of fresh thyme if you have some.

This dish will improve overnight, and is delicious reheated the next day.

Kartoffelpuffer

This is great fun for the whole family. I suggest that everyone sits poised with their forks ready to dig in. Make sure there's plenty to go round, for they will all want more. And more. And more.

2 lb peeled old potatoes	Salt and pepper
1 medium-sized onion	2 oz plain flour
2 eggs	Oil for frying

Grate the potatoes and onion together, mixing thoroughly. Add the eggs and salt and pepper. Heat a tablespoon of oil in a medium-sized, non-stick frying pan and spoon in about three tablespoons of the potato mixture. Spread the mixture well around the bottom of the frying pan and cook on both sides until golden brown and crisp. Serve immediately with salt and lemon juice.

This dish is equally delicious with stewed apple.

Swiss Potato Cake

Slightly more sophisticated this, but an interesting and delicious way to serve potatoes without ruining their flavour. I would like to claim this version of the dish for my own, but I am sure it is a 'second-hand Rose'.

2 lb waxy potatoes	4 oz butter
8 oz Gruyère cheese	Salt and pepper

Wash the potatoes and boil them for five minutes in their skins. Drain, and allow them to cool before peeling. When you have peeled them, cover them well with some cling film and pop them in the fridge to cool, say for a couple of hours.

Now finely grate all the potatoes, or put them through a food processor. Season with salt and pepper. Grate the cheese.

Melt some of the butter in a frying pan, and place a layer of the potato in it, followed by a layer of the Gruyère cheese, then more potato, and fry until golden brown on each side.

Some Fish Dishes

My fishmonger gets up at 6 am and closes her shop at 6 pm. She is eighty-six, and has been doing this since she was twenty-seven and just married. What a good advertisement for fish! How marvellous it would be if the fishing industry in this country could get back on its feet again, and we all got out of the habit of buying frozen fish.

The four recipes that follow can be served as main courses or, by adapting the size of the portions, they would make a delicious starter to a meal.

'Tynesider'

The Geordie is a proud man, and justly so. Over the years he has survived the rough, tough pressures of living in the hard-pressed North-east, and has survived with flair and great good humour.

This dish, named for the old lifeboat 'Tynesider' and her crews who saw over forty years' service on the Tyne, was created by chef Bryan Hodgson. It is bound to please the curious and adventurous eater, so 'when the boat comes in' try this one.

4 large herring fillets	1 medium-sized onion
1 medium-sized leek	2 oz butter
4 oz mushrooms	6 oz prawns

Pastry: see page 52

Coating
1 egg   4 oz toasted oats
$\frac{1}{4}$ pint milk

Sauce
½ pint milk   2 oz plain flour
2 oz butter   2 tbsp English mustard

Clean the herring fillets in salt water, remove scales, and dry on kitchen paper.

Chop the onion, leek and mushrooms together and fry in the butter, adding the prawns (thawed, if frozen) and cook together over a gentle heat for one minute.

Divide the pastry into four and make into rectangles with the rolling-pin. Place one herring fillet on each piece of pastry and add a little of the leek and onion mixture to each. Fold pastry over to make a fish-shaped pasty. Baste with the egg and milk mixture and sprinkle with the toasted oats. Bake in a moderate oven for 20 minutes at gas mark 5, 375°F (190°C).

Sauce
Melt the butter slowly in a thick saucepan and add the flour, milk and mustard. Cook gently for five minutes.

Serve the pasties with a little of the sauce.

Cold beer goes very well with this.

Plaice Lavandou

One of my own recipes now. La Lavandou is a delightful place in Var on the Mediterranean coast of France.
I usually manage to spend a good bit of the tail end of
summer down there, eating and creating a few dishes
of my own. On the campsite where we stay I like to
invite groups of people around for a meal while we
are there. This is a dish I surprised them with a couple
of years ago and the locals are still talking about it!
The trouble is, my French isn't very good, so I'm
never sure just what they are saying . . .

8 fillets of plaice	1 medium-sized onion
6 oz crab meat	1 oz butter
6 oz prawns	Salt and pepper
½ pint double cream	Tomato paste
3 egg yolks	

Butter a large oven dish. Roll the plaice fillets into
little drums and place in the dish.

Finely chop the onion and soften them in a little
butter. Remove from the heat and add the cream,
stirring all the time. Gently beat in the egg yolks and
then add the prawns and the crab meat. Return to the
heat and cook for a few minutes. Pour the sauce over
the fish and bake in a moderate oven, gas mark 5,
375°F (190°C), for about 40 minutes.

Plain boiled rice makes a good accompaniment to
this dish.

*This is a delicious way to serve fish. Sole or cod can
be used instead of plaice.*

Sole with Lime Sauce

Another of my own inventions. I got the idea for it while I was eating in a small Moroccan café-restaurant, 'Le Rendezvous', in Paris.

Why eat in a Moroccan restaurant in Paris? Well, as I say, my French isn't all that good . . .

Do be sure to follow the instructions carefully, as limes can do hideous things to cream!

4 fillets of sole	$\frac{1}{2}$ pint single cream
2 egg yolks	1 oz butter
3 limes	4 oz Gruyère cheese (grated)

Butter an oven dish and lay the fillets of sole in it. Whisk the egg yolks and blend with the juice of the limes.

In a thick saucepan heat the cream gently. Remove the pan from the heat and whisk in the egg yolk and lime juice mixture. Pour this mixture over the fish. Sprinkle with the grated cheese and bake for 30 minutes at gas mark 5, 375°F (190°C).

Serve with plain boiled rice.

Green Eel Soup

Another German dish, this time from Schleswig-Holstein. When I received a copy of this recipe recently from Elizabeth Crookenden, I thought that I had never seen it before, but then I was reminded that German neighbours of ours in East Anglia had once given us something similar. Ideally, it is best to serve this with fresh herbs but you can use dried ones, although the colour effect won't quite be so dramatic. Either way, it is delicious.

We really do underestimate the eel in this country. Since my name in fact means 'eel catcher', perhaps I feel an especial affinity for this dish. It is filling enough to make a main course, though the Germans serve it as a starter.

2 lb of eel	5 or 6 juniper berries
Lemon juice	Peppercorns
$\frac{1}{2}$ pint water	Parsley and other fresh
2 glasses of dry	green herbs, chopped
white wine	Rind of 1 lemon
1 bay leaf	Salt
1 sliced onion	

Wash and clean the eel. Cut into chunks, discarding the head and tail. Place in a thick saucepan and cover with the rest of the ingredients. Simmer very gently for 20 minutes.

Remove the eel pieces from the pan and then strain the fish stock. Blend together 1 oz butter and 1 oz flour, pour in the strained fish stock, and stir until the sauce thickens. Blend together one egg yolk and $\frac{1}{4}$ pint of cream and add this to the sauce, along with lots and lots of herbs: chervil, parsley, lemon thyme, sorrel, dill, chives and tarragon. Now pour the green sauce over the eel and serve immediately.

Dishes with Beef

Despite its sometimes outrageous price, beef is still a firm favourite with many. Don't make the mistake of thinking only of the traditional Sunday roast – it is a very versatile meat, and the various cheaper cuts can be used in many simple and nourishing ways.

If you freeze quantities of the Bolognaise sauce I give here, when the starving Rugby team drops in unexpectedly, you can serve them plates of steaming Spaghetti Bolognaise within minutes . . .

Steak and kidney pies and puddings are definitely stoking up foods for the cold weather, and will adequately fill even the largest frame. But try the stews and casseroles as well – you will find them surprisingly subtle in flavour, and their appetising smell will spread throughout the house as they cook.

Steak, Kidney and Oyster Pie

Now to tell you why my American Air Force friends in Suffolk won't forget me for a very long time. We had decided to give David, who was a pilot, and his wife a traditional English Sunday lunch: roast beef with all the trimmings and, to start with, half-a-dozen Colchester oysters each . . . it was a meal we laid on with pleasure, and all ate it with relish – even David, though he was to pay the price later! Unfortunately, he had never had oysters before and didn't know he was allergic to them, and so the next day one of the USAF's largest bomber planes was grounded . . . all because of one little oyster. There must be a moral in that somewhere.

Oysters were, in days gone by, a staple food of the

poor – a far cry from today when they have become a gastronomic delicacy, with an appropriate price-ticket attached. Even in living memory, they were sold widely at seaside resorts and on whelk stalls, without receiving the kind of fuss – not to say reverence – they get in some English restaurants today, and were none the worse for that.

There is, near when I live in Cumbria, an oyster farm which actually exports oysters to France. If you can get hold of them – either fresh or smoked – try adding them to your next steak and kidney pie. It's a traditional combination, and it's quite delicious.

2 lb braising steak (rump is preferable, but expensive)	2 large onions
	1 pint of good beef stock
8 oz ox kidney	1 tbsp plain flour
6 oz oysters (smoked)	Salt and black pepper
or 1 dozen fresh oysters	

Suet pastry

1 lb self-raising flour	Pinch of salt
4 oz suet	2 eggs
4 oz margarine or butter	

Make the pastry. Add the flour and the suet together in a bowl and rub in the butter. Add a pinch of salt and then the well-beaten eggs, a little at a time, until you have a nice dough. Leave in a cool place for a while.

Cut the meat up into reasonable-sized cubes, together with the ox kidney, and toss in the plain flour with a little salt and lots of black pepper. Slice the onions finely and sauté in a little butter until soft, then add the meat to the frying pan and stir well. Transfer to a casserole, add the stock and cook well covered in the oven for 2 hours at gas mark 2, 300°F (150°C). Then allow to cool.

Roll out the pastry, line a large pie-dish with two-thirds of it, and add the cooked meats, together with the oysters. Roll out the rest of the pastry to make a lid, seal well down, and glaze with any remainder of the beaten egg and a little milk. Bake in a moderate oven, gas mark 5, 375°F (190°C), for about 40 minutes until golden brown.

Steak and Kidney Pudding

Watching my father struggle into the warm kitchen from the snow outside after a hard day and night's lambing in the bitter winds of East Anglia, it was always a joy to see his spirits lift when Mother produced one of these very special steamed puddings. So often neglected by today's cooks, they are all goodness and nourishment. Your hungry family will thank you for serving one of these.

1½ lb stewing or rump steak	1 large onion
½ lb ox kidney	Salt and pepper
	¾ pint good stock

Suet Crust Pastry

1 lb plain flour	Salt
8 oz suet	A little water
1 egg	

Make the pastry. Mix together the flour and the suet in a bowl with the egg and salt. Add a little water to bind the pastry together, if necessary. Well grease a 2-lb pudding basin with butter or margarine. Roll out two-thirds of the pastry into a round, and line the basin with it. Reserve the other third for the lid.

Cut the stewing steak up into cubes, discarding any

excess fat. Chop the kidney. Finely slice the onion and add the steak, onion and kidney to the pudding basin in layers. Pour in enough stock just to cover the meat, and then roll out the lid, place over the basin and seal well. Cover with a cloth or a double layer of foil and secure well with string. Place the basin in a large pan half-filled with water and simmer for $3\frac{1}{2}$ hours until the meat is cooked. Make sure the water does not dry up, and *add only boiling water* to the pan.

Beef with Onions

A traditional French way of using up left-over slices of beef which I first tasted in a station café somewhere near the Somme. I find this simple recipe very useful, and often prepare it with a small piece of beef bought especially for the job. Either way, it makes for good eating. I have used salt beef for this as well.

1 lb sliced, cooked beef	$\frac{1}{4}$ pint of good beef stock
3 tbsp butter	1 tbsp wine vinegar
2 large onions	1 lemon
3 tbsp double cream	Salt and pepper to taste

Melt the butter in a pan and gently fry the very finely sliced onions. After about 5 minutes, add the stock and vinegar seasoning, with salt and pepper to taste. Cook for a further 10 minutes or so before adding the lemon juice.

Turn the heat down to very low indeed and add the finely-sliced pieces of beef, together with the cream. Cover with a well-fitting lid and cook very slowly for a further 15 minutes.

Oxtail Stew

Again, a French-inspired dish, but one with an English sting in its tail . . . it's the black pudding that makes all the difference.

2 oxtails	Black pepper
6 oz gammon	1 lb black pudding
2 medium-sized onions	1 bottle of good
4 carrots	Burgundy or other
1 bouquet garni	red wine
Salt	

Soak the oxtails for a few hours and wash thoroughly. Chop into sections if whole. Dice the gammon and sauté in a large casserole dish, and then add the onions, which have been sliced. Add the oxtail to the casserole and then put in the rest of the ingredients except the black pudding. Make sure that there is enough wine just to cover all the ingredients in the pan. Bring the contents of the pan to the boil and then place in a low oven, about gas mark 2, 300°F (150°C), for $4\frac{1}{2}$ hours. Three-quarters of an hour from the end, add the black pudding.

You will be greeted by a most astonishing aroma as you open the casserole at the table.

Spaghetti Bolognaise

One of the oddest things about living in the depths of the Suffolk countryside during the formative years of my childhood was that none of our neighbours was English! One delightful family of Italians moved into their new home close to ours on a Sunday morning.

They spoke as much English as we spoke Italian, but my parents are kind people and helped them with their bits and pieces. We then settled down to our Sunday roast and, hungry as we always were, we saw to it that there was little left over for a sandwich at supper-time. Imagine how we felt when at 3 pm in the afternoon our new neighbours arrived with a vast dish of Spaghetti Bolognaise . . . it was not even tea-time! We did not know the Italian for 'no' . . .

1 lb minced beef	$\frac{1}{2}$ pint stock (made with
1 15-oz tin tomatoes	beef stock cube)
2 tbsp tomato purée	1 glass good red wine
1 large onion	6 oz button mushrooms
Mixed herbs	Salt and black pepper
Garlic clove	2 tbsp oil
2 tbsp plain flour	

Gently fry the finely chopped onion in the oil in a thick saucepan. Increase the heat and add the minced beef, stirring quickly to make sure it browns evenly all over. Add the finely chopped garlic and flour, and stir in well, and then the tinned tomatoes and tomato purée, stirring all the time. Now pour in the $\frac{1}{2}$ pint of stock. Stir well and add the glass of wine, herbs and sliced mushrooms. Season with salt and pepper. Bring to the boil for a minute and simmer for 50 minutes until cooked.

Serve with spaghetti (allow 2 oz per person) which you should cook in 4 pints of boiling water to which you have added a knob of butter or 2 tbsp oil. Feed in the spaghetti and boil rapidly for 12 minutes. Strain in a colander and serve immediately.

The sauce can also be used with the easy-cook lasagne (add a pint of rich cheese sauce) to make another excellent pasta dish.

Beef Casserole with Wine, Herbs and Peppers

This dish, which comes from Provence, is cooked very slowly in a low oven, so that a delicious winey smell gradually fills the house. Beware if a neighbour has just popped in for a cup of sugar when you take the lid off the casserole to check the cooking – one sniff and she'll want to stay for lunch! Better make a little extra each time you prepare this dish, just in case someone calls . . .

2½ lb chuck steak
8 oz smoked gammon
1 pint red wine
1 15-oz tin tomatoes
2 medium-sized onions
1 red pepper
2 medium-sized carrots

2 garlic cloves
2 strips orange peel
1 bay leaf
2 tsp herbs of Provence
Salt and black pepper
2 oz black olives
3 tbsp olive oil

Buy your steak in one piece and cut it up into as many portions as there are people to serve. Heat the olive oil in a thick casserole and brown the pieces of meat on all sides. Remove the meat. Dice the gammon and sauté for a few minutes in the oil, and remove.

De-seed and slice the red pepper. Slice the onions, carrots and cloves of garlic, and fry all the vegetables in the oil until they are soft. Return the beef and gammon to the pan and add the rest of the ingredients, including the wine. Some people prefer to heat the wine in a separate pan, boiling vigorously for about 5 minutes so that all the alcohol has been removed, before adding it to the casserole. Now seal with a couple of pieces of greaseproof paper or foil and put the lid on. Place in a slow oven, gas mark 1, 275°F (140°C), for 4 to 5 hours.

The Versatile Pig

Contrary to popular belief, pigs are the cleanest of animals if looked after properly. I rejoice in the fact that I was brought up on pork that was not factory farmed. The sows and piglets still ranged freely in the open meadows on the farm where my father was a shepherd, making themselves a delightful mud bath now and then, to wallow in in the hot sun.

You may hesitate before trying the recipe for brawn that I give here, or the Suffolk-cured ham, but I do urge you to have a go. The recipes really are not difficult, and I'm sure a good local butcher who knows his trade will be able to help you with a few hints.

They say of the pig that you can use every part of it except the curl in its tail. I must think of a recipe for that one day!

Himmel und Erde (Heaven and Earth)

Another German dish. I'm not sure when this one first appeared in my collection. I do know, though, that it has many variations in different parts of northern Europe, but this one is very tasty, and really quite cheap.

2 large onions	2 tbsp brown sugar
2 lb potatoes	2 tbsp lard
2 lb cooking apples	$1\frac{1}{2}$ lb pork sausages

Slice the onions and sauté them in the lard. Quarter the peeled potatoes and add to the onions. Add about half a pint of hot water and cook together for about

15 minutes. Then add the peeled and quartered apples, together with the sugar and salt, and cook until the mixture can be easily mashed. Slice the sausages diagonally and fry until brown.

On a dish make a large mound of the apple and potato mixture, and then top with the sausages.

Serve with a green salad.

Stuffed Bacon Chops

Although it may be difficult to get hold of bacon chops in some parts of the country, they are frequently found in some of the larger supermarkets, so I suggest that you persist. Usually a mild-cured back bacon, they should be about half an inch thick.

6 boneless bacon chops (quite thick ones, if possible)	1 large egg
	Juice of 1 lemon
	Salt and pepper
1 small onion, finely chopped	1 large cooking apple
	$2\frac{1}{2}$ oz butter
4 oz fresh breadcrumbs	1 large onion, for garnish
$1\frac{1}{2}$ tbsp sultanas	

Fry the onion in 2 oz of butter for a few minutes and then add the grated apple, breadcrumbs, sultanas, egg, lemon juice and salt and pepper. Mix together well.

Make an incision in the chops and stuff some of this mixture inside them. Lay the chops on a baking tin and place in a moderate oven, gas mark 5, 375°F (190°C), for about 30 minutes. You may need to baste them with a little butter.

While they are cooking, cut the other onion into large rings and fry them in the remaining $\frac{1}{2}$ oz of butter. Use to garnish this dish.

Pork Chop with Bitter Orange and Ginger Sauce

Having been told that bitter oranges were formerly used a great deal in cooking instead of lemons, I decided to put it to the test. I hope you'll agree that, combined with a little ginger, the results are appetising!

1 pork chop per person	1 large carrot
1 oz butter	1 pint strong stock
1 medium onion, finely chopped	1 oz cornflour
Zest of 1 Seville orange	Salt and pepper
2 oz preserved stem ginger	

Trim the fat off the chops. Fry gently in a little butter and put on one side. Finely slice the orange zest, ginger, carrot and onion, add to the pan and fry gently. When they are soft, add the stock and return the chops to the pan, seasoning with salt and pepper. Place in a moderate oven, gas mark 5, 375°F (190°C), for one hour. Remove the chops to a hot dish, and thicken the sauce with the cornflour after adjusting the seasoning. Pour sauce over the chops.

These go well with baked jacket potatoes.

Fillet of Pork Normandie

I have adapted this dish quite considerably since I first tried it out some years ago. It was much more basic then! I hope you will enjoy it in this form.

2 lb fillet of pork
1 lb onions
1 lb cooking apples
  (Bramleys preferably)
1 dessertspoon dried
  sage
¾ pint strong dry cider

1 wine-glass of Calvados
  (if you have it)
1 small carton soured
  cream
1 egg yolk
1 oz butter

Cut the fillet of pork into 3-inch chunks. Melt the butter in a thick oven-proof pan and brown them all over. Put on one side. Slice the onions and peel and core the apples. Cut the apples into quarters. Gently fry the onions until soft, place the pork on top of them, then the apples, sage and seasoning. Cover with cider and cook in a moderate oven, gas mark 5, 375°F (190°C), for 1½ hours until tender. Remove the pork to a warmed dish. Beat together the egg and the soured cream, and add to the sauce in the pan. Finally, add a glass of Calvados. Simmer for a few minutes and then pour over the pork.

This is a full-flavoured dish.

Pork Pie

The first of three family recipes. Although my mother was a good Yorkshire woman by birth, her family were German butchers by origin: her maiden name was Hambrecht. Her mother died when she was young, and she was left to bring up her brothers. She was – and still is – a very good cook. Her recipes are well-tried and tested family favourites which she has passed on to me. I well remember the appetising smells in the kitchen when she was at work.

$1\frac{1}{2}$ lb coarsely minced pork (shoulder or leg)
1 tbsp salt
Salt
$\frac{1}{4}$ tsp nutmeg
1 dessertspoon dried marjoram

Pork bones and two pig's trotters for stock (about 2 lb). This should be made in advance – see recipe.

Pastry
8 oz lard
$\frac{1}{4}$ pint water
1 lb plain flour

$\frac{1}{2}$ tsp salt
$\frac{1}{4}$ tsp bicarbonate of soda

I think I ought to start with a particular word about the stock. Put the bones and the pig's trotters into a large saucepan, along with some salt, pepper and two large onions. You can add a carrot or two as well, if you like. Cover with water and simmer away for some hours.

The pastry is the most complicated part. Put the lard in the water and bring to the boil. Put the rest of the dry ingredients into a large bowl and make a well in the middle. Pour in the liquid and stir until cool and firm. Keep in a warm place for about half an hour. Roll out two-thirds of the pastry to line a 2-lb cake-tin, reserving one-third for the lid. Make sure the tin has a loose bottom.

Mix together the minced pork, salt, nutmeg and marjoram, to make the filling. Pack into the pastry-lined tin. Roll out the lid and place on top, making a generous hole in the middle for the steam to escape. Bake in a moderate oven, about gas mark 4, 350°F (180°C), for just over two hours.

Meanwhile, strain the stock well through two layers of muslin, making sure it is as clear as possible. When the pie is cooked, fill it with stock through the hole in the centre, and allow it to cool well before removing from the tin.

Brawn

Don't let yourself be put off by this one. It really is delicious with brown bread and butter and English mustard, and is not as difficult to make as you may think. But you will need to have an obliging butcher.

1 pig's head	1½ lb shin of beef
4 pig's trotters	Salt and pepper
1 pig's tail	Marjoram
1 pig's tongue	Sage

Soak the pig's head over-night in a little slightly salted water.

In a very large saucepan put all the meat, adding lots of salt and black pepper, some marjoram and some sage. Cook very slowly until the meat begins to fall off the bones.

Remove all the bones and put the meat in a clean bowl, except for the tongue. Mash together energetically. Taste to see if the seasoning needs adjusting. Take the tongue, skin it, and curl it up in the bottom of a large basin. Place the mashed up meat on top, but beware not to pack it down too tightly. Take some of the stock the meat was cooked in (straining it first), and pour it into the basin. It will set to form a delicious jelly, holding the meat together. You will probably still have quite a lot of filling left over, so have several smaller basins ready just in case. It is difficult to give precise quantities because – like humans – pigs' heads vary in size!

Suffolk Sweet Pickle Cure for Bacon and Ham

This recipe should only be attempted during the cold winter months. It is not for those in a rush, or the timid. A cellar in an old house makes an ideal place for the curing process.

1 side of pork	2 oz salts prunella
3-lb bag of salt	(if available)
1 lb saltpetre	2 lb black treacle

Crush all the salts well together. Push as much as you can into the bone of the joint and put the rest with the treacle into a large saucepan. Heat over a gentle flame. Try and dissolve as much of the salts as possible, but don't worry if you don't dissolve them all.

Place the pork, or pieces of pork, in a small tin bath, if you have one. If not, a plastic baby bath will do as well. Lay the pork with the skin downwards and spoon the salt solution generously over. In a day or so you will find that all the salts have dissolved quite happily. Keep the pork in this liquid for one month and baste it each day, turning it occasionally. After one month, remove the pork from the salts and dry thoroughly with a towel. Then hang in a dry, airy room for about three months. A muslin bag or old pillow-case will keep away the flies. The skin and the meat will have turned a very beautiful dark brown by the end of this time. To help dry the bacon out, dust with plain flour from time to time.

Some Lamb Dishes

Here are some new, as well as some traditional recipes for lamb that I have often served to guests at my table in the Close – with delicious results.

Westmorland Lamb Pies

One of the pleasures of living in different parts of Great Britain, as I have done, is the variety of local dishes to be sampled – I'm thinking of Blue Vinny cheese and Dorset Knobs, very special biscuits, from Dorset, for example. The Westmorland Pies given here are a delight, and are excellent served on picnics. This is just one of many recipes that exist for them.

Pastry
12 oz plain flour
$\frac{1}{2}$ level tsp salt

$4\frac{1}{2}$ oz lard
6 tbsp hot water

Filling
8 oz minced lamb
6 oz cooking apples
  (Bramleys preferably)
1 lemon
4 oz currants
4 oz sultanas

4 oz raisins
Pinch of nutmeg and
  cinnamon
Black pepper and salt
Egg for glazing

Make the pastry and keep in a warm place.

Grate the apples. Mix together with all the other ingredients for the filling.

Divide the pastry into about eight portions. Take a 1-lb jam jar, and mould each portion of pastry around the base of the jar, reserving one-third for the lid. Remove the jar, and fill each pie mould with some of the meat mixture. Roll out the lids, and cover the pies, making a generous hole in the centre of the lid.

Glaze each pie with beaten egg and bake in a hot oven, gas mark 7, 425°F (220°C), for 15 minutes, and then reduce the heat to gas mark 4, 350°F (180°C), for a further 15 minutes.

Allow to cool and, if you have any stock, pour a little into each pie.

Serve quite cold with redcurrant jelly.

Swiss Lamb Chops

Although this is a traditional Swiss recipe from the Alps, it was a Swedish lady who suggested the addition of ground allspice to me! It is a simple way to dress up a lamb chop – that is, if you feel it needs it . . .

6 lamb chops	1 oz melted butter
6 oz Gruyère cheese	1 tsp ground allspice
1 clove garlic	

Make an incision in the lamb chops and rub them inside and out with the garlic. Sprinkle a little allspice inside and out, and insert a slice of the cheese in each incision. Baste with the butter and cook under a hot grill until brown.

Lamb Goulash

In Suffolk, on the estate where I lived as a boy just after the war, we still had horses, and if you have working horses you need blacksmiths. I remember that many of these men were Hungarians and Poles who had left their homelands to fight, and now could not return. They could do magical things with metal, and I remember watching with amazement how gently these men would handle the great Shire horses to shoe them. No less skilled in the traditional crafts of their homelands were their wives, and here is a recipe that one of them gave to some friends of mine, who passed it on to me. I think you will find it interesting, to say the least.

2 lb lean lamb	1 15-oz can tomatoes
1 lb onions	1 dessertspoon tomato
2 oz lard or dripping	purée
6 oz pepperoni sausage	$\frac{1}{2}$ pint stock
1 clove garlic	Salt
1 tsp caraway seeds	Black pepper
1 rounded tbsp paprika	2–3 tbsp soured cream
1 level tbsp plain flour	or yoghurt

Cube the meat. Melt the fat in a thick saucepan and then brown the meat. Remove, and add the sliced onions. Fry until tender, and then allow them to brown. Pound together the garlic and the caraway seeds and add to the onions in the pan, together with the paprika and flour. Stir well and then add the tinned tomatoes, tomato purée, the sliced pepperoni sausage, and then the meat. Add the stock, and season well with salt and pepper. Allow to cook on top of the stove for $2\frac{1}{2}$ to 3 hours. Just before serving, stir in the soured cream or the yoghurt.

Try serving this with noodles.

Le Tricolor

This is a dish for that special occasion, rather than the familiar Sunday roast. I hope you will enjoy this unusual combination of meats – the flavour of the turkey is deliciously enhanced by the cooking juices of the lamb. It is something I discovered myself, after some experimentation, and once when I served it, it was greeted with joyous applause!

1 boned shoulder (or
   breast) of lamb
1 turkey breast
2 slices of gammon

2 cloves garlic
1 sprig rosemary
Salt and pepper

Sauce
1 oz butter
1 oz plain flour
Salt
$\frac{1}{2}$ tbsp chopped parsley

2 tbsp brandy
$\frac{1}{2}$ pint chicken stock
$\frac{1}{4}$ pint double cream

Flatten the lamb with a rolling-pin or meat-hammer, and rub with the crushed garlic. Wrap the turkey breasts in the gammon. Place the gammon and turkey, with the sprig of rosemary and the garlic, inside the lamb. Roll up, and bind together with string. Cook in moderate oven, gas mark 5, 375°F (190°C), for $1\frac{1}{2}$ hours.

Sauce
After cooking meat, remove from pan and keep warm. Add butter and flour to the juices, with some salt. Cook on top of the stove for one minute. Add parsley, brandy and stock. Thicken by cooking in pan and reducing. Take pan off the heat and stir in cream. Place in a sauce boat and serve with the meat.
   Spectacular.

Poultry and Game

The importance of a good chicken stock can't be stressed too much, so I make no apology for including a recipe for one. The other chicken recipes were, in one way or another, inspired by visits to France.

It is natural for me to want to include in any recipe book a few game recipes, as I was brought up in Suffolk to live as much as possible off the land, and I still appreciate all the good things the countryside yields. The squeamish, who may flinch from eating hare, venison or pigeons, will want to skip these recipes – but they do taste exceptionally good, if you are prepared to try them.

A Good Chicken Stock

For years I was content to use those little stock cubes, and jolly useful they are, too. However, I must admit I am left with a conscience about all those chicken bones that I discarded so wastefully.

The carcass – skin, bones and liver, heart, etc – of a chicken	Salt
	Black pepper
	Bouquet garni
1 medium-sized onion	Celery, if you have some
2 carrots	Water
1 head of garlic	

Don't bother to peel the carrots or the onion. Just quarter them and add them to all the chicken left-overs in a thick pan, together with the rest of the ingredients. Just cover with water and simmer away on a low heat for a couple of hours. But keep an eye on

it – when it has reduced by half, strain and cool.
You may freeze the stock for future use.

Chicken Provençal

I do like using olive oil. I bought some of the best –
and the cheapest – that I have ever had in the little
market at the foot of the Old Palace in Monaco. It
came in an unlabelled, roughly-corked bottle, having
been poured from a wooden barrel before my eyes. I
go back to Monaco each year when I am on holiday
in the south of France to refill my bottles.

Chicken Provençal is a dish that I enjoy making on
my annual camping holiday.

6 chicken joints
4 tbsp olive oil
2 medium-sized onions
4 tbsp brandy
$\frac{1}{2}$ pint chicken stock
$\frac{1}{2}$ pint dry white wine
2 large cloves garlic,
   finely chopped

1 15-oz tin tomatoes
1 dessertspoon tomato
   purée
1 level tsp herbs of
   Provence
6 oz black olives
1 red pepper

Slice the onions and pepper. Sauté the chicken joints
in the olive oil, along with the garlic. Remove the
joints and fry the onions, tomatoes and pepper.
Return the chicken joints, pour over the brandy, and
flame. Add the rest of the ingredients, except the
olives which should be added 10 minutes before
serving. Simmer the dish on top of the stove for
about an hour until the chicken is tender. Remove the
joints to a hot dish and keep warm. Now boil the
sauce rapidly until it is reduced by half. Pour over the
chicken and serve with plain boiled rice.

Chicken Apricot Pepper

I enjoy the slot I do each Saturday morning for BBC Radio Cumbria on the *It's Saturday* programme. Sometimes, though, I start to panic when I realise at about 11.30 at night that I have not prepared the dish for the next day. This is how I stumbled across this idea, and I think you will find it is very tasty indeed ... I must admit that I had the green peppercorns to hand only because I had been to Paris the week before and had a mad spin around the Galeries Lafayette just before returning to England.

6 chicken joints	A little salt
1 pint good chicken stock	1 oz cornflour
1 medium-sized onion	A little cold water
1 lb cooked dried apricots	1 oz butter
1 dessertspoon green peppercorns	

Melt the butter in a thick saucepan and brown the chicken joints a little all over. Remove from the pan, add the finely-chopped onion and cook until soft. Make a purée of the apricots and add to the pan, together with the chicken stock and the green peppercorns. Simmer gently on the top of the stove for about 45 minutes. Remove the chicken joints and place on a warmed dish. Mix a little cold water with the cornflour and add to the stock. Cook until it has thickened a little. Pour the sauce over the chicken joints.

Serve with plain boiled rice.

Birk Hall Excursion Pie

Mrs D. Langston of Warwick wrote to tell me of this pie, similar to the one of which Tennyson wrote:

There on a slope of orchard, Francis laid
A damask napkin wrought with horse and hounds:
Brought out a dusky loaf that smelt of home,
And half cut down, a pasty costly made.
Where quail and pigeon, lark and leveret, lay like
    fossils
Of the rock, with gold yolks embedded and enjellied . . .

Whether it is the same pie or not, this one is delicious and is particularly good for a picnic or a cold table.

4 grouse or 6 partridges (I use only the breast)	3 medium onions, sliced truffles

Pastry

8 oz flour	1 tbsp water
4 oz butter or lard	1 egg, to glaze
Salt	

Stock

The carcasses of the birds	Carrot
Water, to cover	Bouquet garni
Onion	Garlic clove

Simmer all the stock ingredients together for a couple of hours and then strain.

Make the pastry in the usual way and line an 8-inch cake-tin with it. Fill with the grouse or partridge breasts, onions and truffles, in layers. Pour on the cold stock. Bake in the oven at gas mark 4, 350°F (180°C), for 1½ hours, and then lower to gas mark 3, 325°F (170°C), and cook for another ½ hour.

Serve cold.

Hare Italien

Hare is often a neglected meat outside the countryside, though I have seen it on sale in one or two butchers in some of the larger towns. You may have to order one specially from a game dealer, however. This dish makes a very pleasant change from the traditional Jugged Hare which some people find a little too rich.

1 hare, jointed	2 oz brown sugar
¼ wine glass vinegar	1 dessertspoon cocoa
2 oz butter	powder
1 large onion	1 pint white stock
8 oz smoked gammon,	Salt and pepper
diced	2 oz almonds and raisins

Melt the butter in a thick saucepan and sauté the pieces of hare. Remove, and gently cook the onion in the fat until it is soft. Return the hare to the pan and add the diced gammon. Season with salt and pepper. Add the stock and simmer gently for about an hour. Mix the vinegar and the sugar together and add to the pan, together with the almonds, raisins and cocoa powder. Simmer together for another ½ hour. Adjust the seasoning and serve.

Pigeon Pie

Canon Paul Goddard, the vicar of Sherborne in Dorset, is the inspiration for this pie. He once wrote a recipe for his local church cookery book which began: 'Take four pigeons . . . preferably from the Abbey roof!' It caused some consternation amongst his parishioners, but appears to have done the trick, since there was very little trouble from pigeons in the roof again!

This is my own recipe for pigeon pie. Once again, you may have to place an order for pigeons with a game dealer, but they are becoming increasingly available, particularly frozen ones.

6 pigeons	1 level dessertspoon
1 onion	cayenne pepper
1 carrot	1 oz butter
1 bouquet garni	1 oz flour
1 wine-glass red wine	Salt and pepper
$\frac{1}{4}$ pint water	12 oz shortcrust pastry
1 large red pepper	1 egg, for glazing

In a large pressure cooker place the pigeon, onion, carrot, bouquet garni, red wine and water. Pressure cook for 20 minutes. Strain off the stock and reserve. Use the breasts of the birds only. Line a pie dish with $\frac{2}{3}$ of the pastry, and layer with the pigeon breasts. Dice the red pepper, and fry in the butter in a thick pan until soft. Then add the cayenne pepper and pour in the stock a little at a time, stirring well until a thickish sauce begins to form.

Pour over the pigeon breasts. Roll out the remaining pastry, and cover the pie. Glaze with egg and milk and bake for 40 minutes in a moderate oven, gas mark 5, 375°F (190°C).

Roast Saddle of Venison

On some estates, both in England and Scotland, venison is being farmed commercially and is a very valuable commodity. A friend of mine lost a large number of his herd quite recently to rustlers. The market for the meat is increasing rapidly, and a great deal is exported, especially to Germany. It is also becoming easier to obtain in this country, small joints as well as sides. A rich meat, it's sometimes of indeterminate age, so a good marinade is very necessary. The tougher you think the meat is likely to be, the longer you should leave it in the marinade, in a cool place.

1 venison saddle	1 lb smoked gammon
Salt and pepper	

Marinade

$\frac{1}{2}$ pint water	1 dessertspoon mustard
$\frac{1}{2}$ pint red wine	seeds
$\frac{1}{4}$ pint wine vinegar	1 dessertspoon
2 carrots	peppercorns
2 medium-sized onions	2 bay leaves
1 head of celery	1 dessertspoon dried
1 parsley root	thyme
1 tbsp juniper berries	

Simmer the ingredients for the marinade together for 15 to 20 minutes. Cool, pour over the venison, and leave to marinate for two or three days.

Take the joint out of the marinade and dry it thoroughly. Cut the gammon into strips and 'lard' the joint. This is like making a rug. You make incisions in the meat and push the gammon strips through, so that it will look a bit like a hedgehog. Sprinkle the joint with salt and pepper and hot butter. Cover closely with foil, and bake in an oven preheated to gas mark 5, 375°F (190°C), allowing 20 minutes per pound, plus 30 minutes. Remove the foil for the last 30 minutes and turn the oven up to gas mark 6, 400°F (200°C).

Two Recipes for Pastry

'I have trouble with my pastry.'

That is a complaint I often hear when I am doing cookery demonstrations up and down the country. I must admit I can't remember a time when I ever did have trouble with my pastry. To be quite honest, I am not sure what *good* or *bad* pastry actually is. There is *your* pastry and *her* pastry and *my* pastry and *his* pastry, and what does it matter if they all come out a bit different. The family will always eat them, and I bet it will always be Mum's pastry that they remember when they grow up. So here are a couple of my recipes. They tend to break all the rules but they do work . . . I think.

Food Processor Pastry

This is suitable for all those times when you need a really good shortcrust pastry.

8 oz self-raising flour	Pinch of salt
4 oz soft margarine	4 tbsp ice cold water

Place flour, margarine and salt in food processor and blend together for 20–30 seconds. Add the water and continue blending until the dough forms a ball.

It can be used immediately, but is usually better if left wrapped up for half an hour in the refrigerator.
Can be frozen as well.

A Special Pastry

1 lb 6 oz plain flour   1 tsp salt
1 tsp baking powder   1 tbsp vinegar
1 lb lard   1 cup (5 fl oz) cold milk
1 egg

Blend lard, flour and baking powder. Beat the egg and
add to milk, vinegar and salt. Squeeze together all
ingredients. Leave to stand in a cool place for an hour
before using.

Puddings...The Last Word

Once upon a time I thought I did not have a sweet tooth, but like my dislike of broad beans, I grew out of it. Even so, I feel we overdo the pudding and desserts a little – to be honest, I think I prefer illicitly nibbling the left-overs after everybody has gone! That way you can confine yourself to an apple or an orange at the end of the meal, and pride yourself on your self-abstinence – the truth being that during the cooking you were tasting this and nibbling that, so that you really can't manage anything more . . . but a little later, when they have all gone home, you can forget the waistline and indulge a little . . .

Yorkshire Curds

Once again, a remembered taste from childhood, and one that is asked for time and again. It does take a little time to prepare this dish, but it is well worth the effort. In Yorkshire, as I suspect in many parts of the north of England, they still have a baking day. If this dish were baked first, it would probably have to be repeated again towards the end of the day – little fingers would have wandered away with giant-sized slices!

For the curds
1 quart milk   1 tbsp vinegar
1 dessertspoon plain flour

6 oz sugar
6 oz currants   Pinch of nutmeg
1 oz melted butter   8 oz shortcrust pastry
1 egg

The day before, heat the milk until a skin just forms and then stir in the flour and the vinegar until it turns to curds. Take off the heat and strain through a muslin bag over-night, until all the juices have run away.

In the morning, mix with all the other ingredients. Roll out the pastry and line a flan case with it. Pour in the mixture and grate some nutmeg over the top. Bake on the bottom shelf of the oven at gas mark 7, 425°F (220°C), until firm and golden brown.

A little rum can be added for a better flavour.

Tombstone Pudding

I have Mrs Jane Tookey of Wells in Somerset to thank for this recipe. Her husband is the priest at the church of St Thomas, Wells. It is a rich pudding, and I love to watch people's faces when I tell them its name just as they are about to put a spoonful in their mouths. Don't be put off, though – it is very good.

2 packets sponge fingers	2 tbsp water
4 eggs	A little rum or sherry
6 oz butter	Whipped cream and
4 oz caster sugar	crystallised violets for
4 oz plain chocolate	decoration

Dip the sponge fingers in sherry or sugared, watered rum, and arrange to stand on end around a glass bowl or serving dish. Cream the butter and sugar, and melt the chocolate and water over a pan of hot water. Separate the eggs and beat the yolks until light and fluffy. Add to the butter mixture and then beat in the chocolate. Whip the egg whites until stiff but not 'dry', and fold into the mixture. Pour into the serving dish and chill. Decorate with whipped cream and crystallised violets.

Jamaican Chill

Sylvia Restall of the Vicarage at Reading in Berkshire has sent me this very appetising recipe. I have varied her quantities a little. I must admit that I have a dreadful weakness for raisins, rum and chocolate. It is difficult not to keep making this every Sunday.

8 trifle sponge cakes	5 fl oz rum
4 oz butter	4 oz raisins
4 oz caster sugar	4 oz chopped nuts
4 eggs	

Line a 2-lb loaf tin with foil. Cut the sponges into fingers. Cream together the butter and the sugar, and then beat in the egg yolks one at a time, beating well. Whip the egg whites until they are really thick and stiff and fold into the butter mixture. Cover the bottom of the tin with a layer of sponge. Sprinkle with the rum. Spoon over some of the cream filling, and then sprinkle with the nuts and raisins. Repeat the process, building up the layers of sponge and cream, until all the ingredients have been used up. Cover in foil and press down with a weight of some kind. Chill very well in the fridge, or keep in the freezer for up to four weeks. Invert onto a dish and decorate with glacé cherries, cream and angelica.

A tip! I left the raisins to soak in a quantity of rum over-night. But then I would!

Dominic

This dish gets its name because Dominic turned up at the right time, just as I was looking for something a little unusual to serve as a chilled sweet. I can't re-member how we arrived at kiwi fruits. When I demonstrated this recipe in public at Cheynes Manor in Buckinghamshire, the result was stunning. Very simple and oh, so different.

5 or 6 kiwi fruits	2 limes
2 oz sugar (caster preferably)	$\frac{1}{2}$ pint double cream

Peel the kiwi fruit and chill. Place in a food processor or blender with the sugar, the finely grated rind of one of the limes and the juice of both. Purée the contents. Beat the double cream until it peaks and then fold into the mixture.

Serve well chilled in tall wine glasses, with brandy snaps.

Apricot and Ginger Ice

This recipe is another that came to me late one night, when I wanted a break from writing the sermon for Sunday. It was about 2 am in the morning – not that I usually burn the midnight oil over sermons, but I had been to a pop concert in Newcastle.

2 cans apricot halves	4 oz stem ginger
1 lemon	(preserved in sugar)
7 oz caster sugar	$\frac{1}{2}$ pint double cream

Place the contents of one of the cans of apricots, with the juice, in a food processor or blender. Add the apricots from the other can, reserving the juice. Squeeze the lemon and add the juice to the food pro-cessor, with the caster sugar, stem ginger and double cream. Process or blend until the mixture is fairly smooth, and then freeze.

Serve the ice with the left-over juice of the apricots and a little finely-chopped ginger.

This has a delicious flavour, and would be just as good made with dried apricots which have been soaked and cooked, and then left to chill over-night. You would need about 1 lb of dried fruit. However, this is the quick way and does save a lot of time.

Belfry Trifle

Whenever I make this trifle, they seem to be practising the bells in the Cathedral . . . Have you ever lived next door to a church where they have fanatic bell-ringers? Actually, I love the sound of the bells and would miss them dearly if they were not rung – I certainly would be in danger of missing the 10.30 service on a Sunday morning without them! However, back to the trifle. I have made this one for years, and everyone has said it is a must for the book. So here it is. Enjoy it.

1 packet trifle sponges	1 lb raspberry jam
1 large can good quality fruit cocktail	2 cups sweet sherry

Custard

1½ pints milk	Vanilla pod
6 egg yolks	1 pint double cream
4 oz caster sugar	

Spread the trifle sponges with raspberry jam and place at the bottom of a deep dish. Pour the large can of fruit cocktail over, and then the sherry.

To make the custard, gently heat the milk with the

vanilla pod in it. Beat together the eggs and sugar and, when the milk is about lukewarm, add them to it, stirring continuously until the mixture begins to thicken. Allow to cook for about a minute, and then pour over the contents of the dish. Chill well, and when the custard has set, whip the double cream and apply liberally to the top.

Decorate, if you like, with chopped walnuts.

Mère Catherine

If you climb up to the Sacré Coeur in Paris and then turn left, you come to la Place du Tertre – the little square full of restaurants, where artists and tourists gather. It is a fascinating place. The restaurants vary tremendously, and this dish is named after the one where I first sampled something similar, which gave me the inspiration to try it for myself.

It was an enchanting evening, with a violinist and a pianist, and excellent company. After dinner, we wandered around the square and my friends had their portraits drawn by one of the artists there.

7 oz white chocolate	4 oz caster sugar
$\frac{3}{4}$ pint double cream	Chopped nuts
4 egg yolks	A little orange liqueur

Melt the chocolate in a bowl over a pan of hot water. Blend together the egg yolks and the sugar until light and fluffy. Heat the cream gently in a thick saucepan until it is almost boiling. Whisk half the hot cream into the eggs, and then pour all into the pan with the rest of the cream, stirring until the custard mixture thickens slightly.

Take the custard off the heat and stir in the melted

chocolate and beat well. Now pour the mixture into an ice cream churn, if you have one, but don't worry if you haven't. You should place the mixture in a plastic bowl, cover it and put it in the freezer. Look at it after an hour. If ice crystals are beginning to form, stir the custard with a wooden spoon or silver fork to break down the ice, then allow it to freeze again. Repeat the process if you feel that too much ice is forming.

When it has frozen, divide the ice cream up into ramekins or small metal sponge cups and freeze again for a while. Remove the ices from the cups and roll in the warmed, chopped nuts. Place in the freezer on a tray, and cover until required.

Just before serving, place on a dish and pour over a quantity of orange liqueur. Set alight.

Serve immediately.

Summertime

This is a superb dish that takes months to make. You need to start with the first fresh soft fruits of the summer. Ideally you need a tall stone jar with a wide mouth, something about the size of one of those sweet jars that you used to see in corner shops – though if you did use a glass jar, you would need to black out the sides and keep out of the sunlight.

Various fresh fruits and berries, such as: raspberries, black-currants, redcurrants, brambles, strawberries, blueberries, and any other succulent fruit	1 bottle rum Brown sugar

Over the summer period, build up layers of fruit, about 1 lb a layer, followed by a layer of brown sugar, about 4 oz a layer, and then top up with the rum. Repeat the process as more fruit becomes available, noting on the side of the jar how the layers are built up, and making sure the liquid covers the fruit. Keep the lid of the container well sealed.

Serve with fresh cream in the depths of winter.

Stollen

This is a traditional cake from Germany. I remember Mrs Bayfield, one of our neighbours in Norfolk who was from Germany, making it. I recently came across it again by a swimming pool in the Lake District! I have made a few adaptations to the recipe as given me, and I think you will find it works very well. It keeps excellently – if you can resist eating it all at once. It also goes well with the Firetongs Punch.

2 lb strong plain flour	Allspice
4 oz yeast	8 oz chopped almonds
$\frac{3}{4}$ pint milk	6 oz raisins
6 oz light brown sugar	6 oz currants
Vanilla pod	6 oz sultanas
12 oz butter	6 oz mixed peel
1 lemon	$\frac{1}{4}$ bottle rum, brandy,
Salt	whisky or port, etc.
Mixed spice	

Soak the raisins and other fruit in the rum or whichever liqueur you use.

To make the yeast dough, have everything as near as possible to room temperature. Mix the yeast with a little lukewarm milk, add the sugar and leave for half an hour in a warm place. Put the flour in a large warmed bowl and make a well in the middle. Pour the yeast into the well and gently mix into the flour, adding the softened butter as you go. Knead into an elastic dough which is clean and promising. Now knead in the fruit and the spices. This will require a lot of patience, and perhaps a little more flour. Now cover the bowl and place in a warm place until it is well risen. Then knead again to get all the air out of it.

Have ready a buttered baking tray. Shape the dough into an oval, place on the tray and leave to rise again. Cover with buttered greaseproof paper and place in an oven at gas mark 6, 400°F (200°C), for about an hour, and then lower the temperature to gas mark 2, 300°F (150°C), for about half an hour. Test with a skewer to see that it is cooked.

Remove from the oven. Brush with melted butter and dust with icing sugar.

The cake will keep for about two weeks if kept in an airtight container.

Firetongs Punch

It works, it really does. This is another recipe given me by Elizabeth Crookenden, and she has told me how she used to watch her father make it in their home on the continent. You do have to keep the rum away from the flame, just in case the flame jumps. It is a superb drink for a cold winter evening.

1 sugar loaf, weighing
  ½ lb
1¾ pints red wine
A few cloves

A cinnamon stick
Rind of 1 lemon
Juice of 2 oranges
A quantity of rum

Heat the wine, cloves, cinnamon, lemon rind and juice of two oranges together, but do not allow to boil.

Make sure your firetongs are clean, and balance them across the top of the pan containing the heated wine. Lower the lights, and balance the sugar loaf on the tongs. Gradually drip some of the rum onto the sugar loaf and apply a match As the sugar loaf burns, it will drop into the wine. Keep spooning the rum onto the sugar loaf until it has all been dissolved and burnt away.

Serve this delicious concoction in heatproof glasses.

Le Grand Gâteau

This really is the last word . . . it is outrageously extravagant and – well, enough is enough, but it will serve over 25 people if made in this quantity. It is a dish I have made for special occasions and have been amazed to discover how many people, having seen me make one, have actually gone on to make one for their own parties.

Try it . . . if you dare.

(I wonder if it should carry a Government health warning?)

3 large flan cases
1 lb icing sugar
$\frac{1}{2}$ lb butter
2 oz cocoa powder

2 lbs black cherry
   conserve
4 pints double cream
$\frac{1}{4}$ bottle whisky

Make a rich butter icing by blending together the icing sugar, butter, cocoa powder and about half the whisky. When this mixture is smooth, fill one of the flan cases with it. Place another of the flan cases on top and fill this one with the black cherry conserve.

On top of this, add some of the double cream that has been whipped until it is very thick (about $\frac{1}{2}$ pint of double cream should be enough). Then invert the final flan case on top of the cream and jam-filled flan case – just like putting on a hat. Now the real job begins. Heap the rest of the cream, all 5 pints of it, on top and spread it all over the cake.

There you have it – Le Grand Gâteau. It should serve between 25 and 30 people, and is really superb for buffets and large gatherings.